REST *in* PEACE

Insider's Tips to the Low Cost Less Stress Funeral

R. BRIAN BURKHARDT

NEW Y

D1409995

REST *in* PEACE

By R. Brian Burkhardt
© 2008 R. Brian Burkhardt. All rights reserved.

ISBN: 978-1-60037-398-5   Paperback

Published by:

MORGAN · JAMES
THE ENTREPRENEURIAL PUBLISHER™

Morgan James Publishing, LLC
Heather@GraphicsByHeather.com
1225 Franklin Ave Ste 325
Garden City, NY 11530-1693
Toll Free 800-485-4943
www.MorganJamesPublishing.com

Cover and Interior Design by:
Heather Kirk
www.GraphicsByHeather.com

Peninsula
Building Partner

CONTENTS

PART I
PLAN IN ADVANCE
TO STAY IN CHARGE

PART II
EMPOWERING YOUR ARRANGEMENTS

REST *in* PEACE

IV

PART III
FUNERAL COST
FLASHPOINTS

CONTENTS

V

PART IV

HOW-TO: EXAMPLES OF LOW COST, NO COST (!?!), LESS STRESS FUNERALS

REST *in* PEACE

VI

ACKNOWLEDGMENTS

To be consistent with the rest of the book, I am going to give many people thanks here without naming names.

First of all, to my wife and two children, thanks for all your love and kindness, to R. Brian, the Funeral Director and Author.

Thanks to the former reporter from the *Chicago Daily News*, without his help this book could not have been written.

To all the funeral directors I have worked with…thanks for all I am learning and have learned.

To my coaches and mentors your encouragement has been wonderful.

To the web designer who has given time without charge, eternal thanks.

To my fellow ezminisiters who helped give birth to this project, great thanks.

To the one who gave the speech "talent is not enough," your inspiration was priceless.

To my personal physician, thanks for saving my life.

To the hospital technician who went above and beyond her duties and discovered a life threatening situation, you are my hero.

To all my internet marketing friends, many thanks.

To all the families I have served as a funeral director,God bless you.

For all those prayers from all over, thanks for your help in this great adventure.

My first day of funeral service was on September 11, 2001. Peace to all the families grieving about that day. We will never, never forget.

To all who read this book, thanks for lowering the cost of your funerals.

FOREWORD

Everyone has heard the old saying that in life there are two constants., death and taxes. There are tax strategies we can learn and save our money. Recently I have learned there are funeral strategies where we can save money at the vulnerable moment. These strategies leave more money for the living.

The information here astonished me. These pages present practical cost savings. R. Brian has shared this excellent content with me. He has lived what he has written. One does not have to spend thousands of extra dollars to move on to the next life with dignity and honor.

This consumer guide presents money saving strategies and how to tips on lowering the cost of your funeral. Not only does the author walk you through the funeral process, he demystifies the funeral and lowers the cost of every funeral you may be involved in the business back end. YOU ARE HOLDING IN YOUR HAND A GUIDE THAT SHOULD BE IN EVERY HOME. This work can dramatically save your survivors time, stress, grief, and money when you pass on. This is THE HOW TO MANUAL FOR FAMILIES FOR EVERY FUNERAL.

The information here is the real thing. After asking questions and spending time with the author he emerged the true expert. The tips here go beyond revealing insider secrets for the first time. R.Brian skipped the name calling whistle blowing finger pointing etc. He effectively teaches how to lower the cost and stress of a funeral., any funeral.

I could of told you to be sure not to miss specific sections of the book. Instead take out a pen and paper and take notes. You will find yourself thinking and planning out your legacy. YOU OWE IT TO YOURSELF & YOUR FAMILY TO LOWER YOUR FUNERAL COST. This is a Great Book!

Matt Bacak
Duluth, GA

INTRODUCTION

STREET-WISE MORTALS

The main purpose of this book is to help people to lower the costs and stress related to funerals. The truth is that you can save hundreds or thousands of dollars on a funeral, if you know in advance what's involved and make some wise decisions. Please take the time now to review the subject. Even a casual reading, without an immediate need for the ideas here, will lessen or remove some of the negative images that come to mind with the word "funeral." How good it is to do that before the need arrives.

Rest In Peace will give you a "how-to" on the entire funeral process. Another goal is to help you work with funeral homes and funeral directors. There are many excellent ones. Remember, though, funeral homes are staffed with people. They come with the pluses and minuses-that are part of every individual.

I have the deepest respect and sympathy for anyone facing the thought of losing a loved one. We all face this major life change. While we have a tendency to plan carefully for the changes that encourage and build life goals, we're not as enthusiastic about pursuing other necessary, but less attractive, planning opportunities — like funerals.

When you finish reading, you will be able to make some general and some specific decisions, even now, that will be helpful in the future. Thinking about a funeral and discussing it now is a current act of compassion that will serve you or your loved ones later, when time is compressed and when there may be greater financial and emotional burdens. This book will put you on the path to solving the painful problem of the funeral.

PART I

Plan in Advance to Stay in Charge

1

It's Your Funeral, Plan In Advance To Stay In Charge Mr. (Or Ms.) President

The President's Plan / Why Buy the Ceremony? / Identity Change / In Advance — In Charge /

The President's Plan

When the President of the United States takes office, one of the first jobs the new First Family faces is to plan a state funeral. (Plan in advance, Mr. or Ms. President.) Whether you are William J. Clinton, Democrat, or George W. Bush, Republican, does not make a difference in this process. A notebook is assembled that contains all the details of the plan. Think about the significance of this act of advance planning. At a time of major grief and transition in a family, a country, the world, a plan is in place that will help to bring remembrance, celebration, dignity, stability, balance, unity, and some closure for millions of people.

3

The good news is that you're not planning a state funeral. What a relief.

WHY BUY THE CEREMONY?

It is best to have some kind of ceremony when a loved one dies, even (or especially) if the loved one is cremated. It is better not to try to dispense with grief only by making dust or ashes. The obvious answers for some to the question, "why buy the ceremony," will be to show honor to the one who died, to start the process of bringing closure for people to whatever events led to the loss and, certainly, to start the process of closure for the loss itself.

IDENTITY CHANGE

A less obvious reason for the ceremony is that when a loved one dies, your identity changes. There is a new you. The closer you were to that person, the more your identity may change. In the absence of the loved one, you walk through life differently.

A ceremony invites others to come and support you in your new life and changed circumstances. If you do not have a public ceremony, it may seem to people around you that you are telling them, "I'm just the way I always was. I don't need support." This isn't a helpful message. It does not give people a place to relate to you openly in this new life. It doesn't give them a place to start. We all need supportive relationships — especially at a time of grief as parts of identity shift.

A funeral allows relationships to be renewed, while in community, that reflect the important changes that have occurred. It allows for the expressions of what that person who died and related loved ones have meant to individuals and that community of people who still love and care.

IN ADVANCE — IN CHARGE

The first step to a low cost, less stress funeral is to recognize that *you are in charge.*

The corollary is: *at your funeral, you are only in charge when you plan in advance.*

A basic funeral plan can be completed in a few hours or days, filled in or changed over time, as necessary — like updating an insurance policy. A simple plan and a few choices made *in advance* can save your family and loved ones hundreds or thousands of dollars. The words in advance are the key to maximizing savings on a funeral.

As President of You (plan in advance, Mr. or Ms. President), you make business decisions every day, some of which affect your life dramatically. If you've purchased life or auto insurance, you already know why the words "*in advance*" are important. A plan *in advance* allows you to look around to obtain the best benefits at the least cost. It gives you greatest control over the results. The purchase of a funeral and funeral-related products is a series of business decisions with a heavy emotional component. These choices should be separated as much as possible from the date of the need in order to be thought through clearly.

You probably will need to focus on the business end of a funeral only a few times in your life. So, it may seem like another part of the pain that comes with the territory. (*Just let me sign this contract, with these prices I haven't discussed much with anyone, and get it over with. Maybe it'll come out of the insurance or the estate — I can't deal with this, too. If this is what it costs, this is what it costs. I loved _____.*) Perhaps you thought you were limited to a choice among "complete" packages offered by the funeral home staff or a funeral director. It may not be clear that you have choices in a number of areas regarding funeral costs.

Funeral home personnel will have sensitivity and understanding for your needs. They receive training for that in mortuary school. As with every other industry, there are dedicated, committed, helpful, caring people available to serve you, especially because you pay them and that's the job.

In advance — for funeral savings and a lower funeral cost — happens before you or your shocked, hurting family and loved ones are forced to start making a series of costly decisions, a few moments after a death occurs, while riding heavy emotional waves.

You can rely on the fact that your local funeral home has a plan. Their personal plan for your funeral fits into their business plan. Funerals are big business. It's a $13 billion dollar per year industry, not including billions of dollars in funds sitting around in presold contracts called "preneed" (see that chapter later). Their business plan may have areas that hold little real benefit for you. It's up to you to discern what you really need from them.

At one recent public funeral for a national figure, the casket cost about $20,000. At another recent public funeral for a national figure, the casket cost about $200 (see Part IV of this book). Each ceremony was a heartfelt time of reflection and remembrance that included family, friends, and dignitaries.

You really can have a funeral, at a lower cost, that will accomplish all the goals of a funeral as a dignified memorial of a loved one's life, or your own.

Rest *in* Peace

8

2

TRANSPORTING YOUR LOVED ONE, THE EMBALMING QUESTION & HOW TO ANSWER IT, FIRST DECISIONS FIRST

911 or Code Blue / Transporting Your Loved One (Last Ride in a Van) / Personal Effects / Permission to Embalm? / Embalming and Grief?

911 OR CODE BLUE

The chain of events leading to hiring a funeral director usually starts shortly after the time of death, frequently with a call to 911. Rapidly after medical and legal procedures and reporting occur to satisfy all legal requirements (including possible organ donation), the body will be ready for release to a funeral director.

Transporting Your Loved One (Last Ride in a Van)

In most states, it is the law that a funeral director must come to transport the body of your loved one. The funeral director and/or associate will arrive in a van with a cot. The point at which you call the funeral home to remove the deceased is the first point at which you will be incurring a charge from that business. This removal charge can vary quite a bit, by as much as several hundred dollars, not just based on locality or distance, but also — as with nearly every other cost for funeral goods and services — the price depends on what the market will bear. It will be helpful to have someone present who is emotionally able to handle the circumstances for this transfer, someone who can make the necessary phone calls, and who will have the presence of mind to confirm the cost before the end of the call, if the removal comes under emergency conditions. Frequently the removal is made at the site of a medical facility and that allows more time to work out the details and costs of a removal. But, the removal may also be made from a medical facility with a call by medical personnel to a funeral home after friends or family have left. So, it's possible to become responsible for charges that you didn't authorize directly.

Once your loved one is on the cot, the body is in the funeral director's care. A good funeral director will allow you to view your loved one the next day, as you desire to, without charging. You will want to confirm this before the body is given to the funeral director. The transfer may be made when you are not there. If you later wish to have time with your loved one, and the funeral director tells you there will be a charge, just let the funeral director know that you will need to make a positive identification, at no charge.

PERSONAL EFFECTS

A helpful funeral director who oversees the transfer will make sure all personal effects (gold rings, watches, wallet, hearing aids, etc.) are returned to you before your loved one is transferred. Be cautious — make sure to remove any personal property prior to the transport, otherwise things could become lost during this process.

PERMISSION TO EMBALM?

Even as the removal occurs, the funeral director will begin to ask questions regarding funeral plans that will affect what happens next with your loved one. The funeral director first asks if there will be a closed casket (no embalming required), or an open casket (with embalming). A funeral director may handle this in a slightly different way and just ask, at the time of the transfer, for permission to embalm your loved one. Embalming is a substantial charge, ranging from several hundred dollars to over one thousand dollars.

Embalming and Grief?

Embalming is a very personal decision. It certainly is not a necessity to have a loved one embalmed. Some funeral directors will tell you that you have to embalm a loved one to allow the resolution of grief. It is true that you may need to work through grief over time. It is not true that embalming can resolve grief issues. Grief is a longer process. It begins with the death, but may not be resolved for months or up to a couple of years.

Embalming does not normally preserve the body forever. It allows the body to appear natural in an open casket during a visitation or funeral service. That may bring comfort to some friends and family members.

You can always choose a closed casket burial, or cremation, that will eliminate the embalming charge. People of the Islamic and Jewish faiths have ceremonies that conform to traditions of their respective faiths and do not embalm — or cremate. In Arab countries and Israel, even caskets aren't usually used by these groups. You may have noticed, during the public funeral that was broadcast around the world, that Pope John Paul II was not embalmed.

When the funeral director asks if you want your loved one embalmed, you have the right to say no to this, that you don't want your loved one embalmed.

If you haven't made up your mind about embalming, you have the right to say that you don't want to decide at that moment. That's especially true if you don't have a written price for the service from the funeral director, and also from at least two other reputable funeral homes or trade embalmers in your area. Trade embalmers are licensed, independent contractors who may work for many funeral homes, but also work on individual jobs as freelancers. Experience is the best qualification for this work.

Even if the state or local authority says embalming must occur in 24 hours, you can say, "I need to wait to decide."

Some funeral homes do not have refrigeration equipment — which forces the embalming issue on you. If this is the case, you can tell the funeral director that you cannot decide now and that your loved one should be taken to a refrigerated facility, usually the county morgue, or another funeral home with refrigeration equipment.

As with any other consumer purchase, prices from competitive companies, in this case, funeral homes, are the best protection against paying too much. Your family may need time to discuss this issue together before an embalming decision is made. That's why it's good to decide the embalming question before the need comes.

A good funeral director will have a price list with him when he asks for permission to embalm. Written permission is required to embalm and the funeral director will also have a form for that. Only agree to embalming with written permission that includes a written price.

The cremation rate in the U.S. is expected to average about 36 percent by 2010. The percent of decisions for cremation is somewhat higher in urban areas, lower in rural areas. Cremation is generally less than the cost for a casket funeral, but not always. Recently, the cost of cremation has been rising at many funeral homes, even to equal the price of a whole funeral at other funeral homes. Once again, it's important to obtain additional prices from other funeral homes and other vendors for these goods and services.

If you choose cremation, choose a crematory. The cost of cremation should be lower if this service is not being outsourced by a funeral home that does not have facilities on site.

3

THE FUNERAL AND YOUR ROLE AS THE FUNERAL DIRECTOR

Funerals Then / Funerals Now / Key Points of a Funeral /Changing Role of the Funeral Director

FUNERALS THEN

Funeral services before the Twentieth Century often took place in the family home. In middle and upper class houses, a parlor was a frequent feature that served as a living space for families to host major life events like weddings and funerals. Then, as now, death was viewed as one of the last stops on the full spectrum of life events on earth. Families and loved ones prior to the Twentieth Century had greater proximity to this part of the life journey. They cared for the bathing and dressing of the body (in the same way that these same tasks are performed by families, friends, or burial societies in some religions today). A casket would lie at rest in the household for a few days as a place of visitation, wake, and ultimately the site of the service. Sometimes both the funeral service and even the burial took place at home.

FUNERALS NOW

Traditionally, the funeral home receives a call and makes a trip to transfer the body of the deceased person to the funeral home, where it may be prepared for viewing and placed in a casket for a visitation, a time when others can come and pay respects to the family.

Funeral services usually follow at the funeral home, church, or graveside — and sometimes more than one of these places. Then a casket is taken for burial. If cremation has occurred, the ashes may be placed in a box or other container (such as an urn).

KEY POINTS OF A FUNERAL

The elements of a funeral often include:

- The casket or urn
- The obituary
- Flowers
- The visitation
- The funeral service eulogy, music, and memories or tributes

- The procession to the burial site

- The committal service at the gravesite

- The gathering (of family and friends after the burial for a social time)

CHANGING ROLE OF THE FUNERAL DIRECTOR

Funeral directors came into existence during the Civil War. Many soldiers killed during the war were buried near where they fell. Improvements in embalming at the start of the war made it possible for some soldiers' bodies, for the first time, to be sent home for services and burial.

Funeral directors and doctors also provided exceptional service at the time of the Titanic tragedy. Bodies pulled from the north Atlantic were embalmed on ship deck. Loved ones were sent home to be mourned and buried.

In times of national disaster, there is a need for multitudes of funerals in a shortened time period, like those following September 11, 2001. The work of funeral directors allows bereavement to have its proper display and mourning to start a road toward healing.

The everyday role of the funeral director has been changing over time. Some of the funeral director's functions are not as necessary as they once were. The reality is that today the average person can plan a funeral that reduces the role of the funeral director.

When you look at it more closely, some of what funeral directors do is not very different from event planning. As a wedding planner might be hired to produce a wedding, a funeral director offers a similar kind of coordination through the series of events surrounding the funeral. A funeral, of course, is not as intricate as a wedding, except in its emotional aspects. Frequently, the consumer can take on some of the funeral director's role as event planner.

At the same time, the funeral director offers a complete selection of goods, as well as services, available for purchase. Many of the goods associated with funerals can be purchased outside the funeral home. Many of the services can be performed by family and friends. The more items a family and friends do to "prearrange" for a funeral, the more they can lower the cost of a funeral.

Additionally, the funeral director's role includes coordinating or performing the embalming or cremation of the body. Whether these jobs are coordinated or performed is determined by the equipment available at the funeral home and the licensure of the staff. Funeral homes without these facilities or licensed employees may bring in trade embalmers and outsource cremations. Because embalming and cremations are performed by licensed individuals, it's important to check available pricing from several sources.

The funeral director also serves as the administrator, mandated by law, of certain legal documents, with other paperwork generated by the process. This includes officially signing the death certificate and sending paperwork to report the death to the Social Security Administration.

Because of the changing nature of the business, funeral homes offer "package" deals to maintain as much of their traditional business roles (and revenues) as possible.

In summary, today a consumer can perform more of the functions once assigned to a funeral director than ever before.

CHAPTER 3

PART
II

*Empowering Your
Arrangements*

4

CONSUMER ALERT: YOUR FUNERAL RIGHTS

Exercise The Funeral Rule / The Funeral Bill of Rights / A Warning About Obituaries With TMI / An Example of an FTC Clarification / NFDA and the Funeral Rule / Calling the FTC

EXERCISE THE FUNERAL RULE

In the early 1980s, the Federal Trade Commission (FTC) started to enforce a new body of regulations known as "The Funeral Rule." The purpose of the "Rule" was to protect consumers from unfair practices when purchasing a funeral and funeral related items. The FTC is still responsible for enforcement of the "Rule." Periodically, the Commission writes opinions that help to clarify industry practices with respect to the Funeral Rule. Among other rights given to consumers in the Funeral Rule, it says that you are required only to purchase the goods and services that you want from a funeral home.

More of your consumer rights, most derived from the Funeral Rule, follow below.

THE FUNERAL BILL OF RIGHTS

1. You have the right to know the prices of the Goods and Services you are paying for in advance, at any funeral home, either when you visit, or over the phone, when you call. You do not need to give them your name, address, or other information before they give you the prices you ask for when you phone them.

2. You have the right to see the casket and vault price list when you go into a funeral home and at an arrangement conference. If you are shopping for a funeral you must be shown a casket price list. While some detailed casket information may appear on the list of goods and services, usually funeral homes have a separate written list for casket prices. The funeral home will be sure that you see their most costly caskets first. Before they show you any caskets, be sure that you get a copy of the written list so that you can identify less expensive caskets that would suit your needs, and request to see them.

3. You have the right to negotiate your contract with a funeral director and funeral home.

4. You have the right to choose embalming, cremation, or direct burial. A funeral home director or

agent is obligated to inform you of this right. Sometimes a funeral director or agent may ask instead just for permission to embalm your loved one when the funeral home arrives to transport the body. (See Chapter 2 of this book.)

5. You have the right to bring a casket or urn from another source (including a wholesaler or internet provider) into the funeral home, that will be used to contain the remains of your loved one for display or burial.

6. You have the right not to pay a funeral home an additional fee if you bring in a casket or urn from another source. A funeral home cannot charge you a fee for using a casket/urn from another source and you do not need to be present when it is delivered at the funeral home.

7. You have the right to have services at a different site from the funeral home you have chosen.

8. You have a right to produce the items you need for a funeral service or buy them from another source (other than the funeral home you are using for some goods or services), including: flowers, the Order of Service programs, registration/guest book, memorial folders, prayer cards, and other service related items, as well as electronic media presentations like slide shows and videos.

9. You have the right to write the obituary.

10. You have the right to your funeral service your way. You have the right not to select a "package" from a funeral home's group of packages.

A WARNING ABOUT OBITUARIES WITH TMI (TOO MUCH INFORMATION)

Whether a funeral home writes the obituary, or you do, you need to be careful not to list the full, exact name, address, the date of birth, or other important identifying information. Don't allow this information to be published. The AARP warns that scammers now read obituaries for this information and use it to purchase other information (like Social Security numbers and credit histories) off the Internet. Information is sold to others who illegally make up fake IDs and licenses, then buy cars or open credit accounts in the dead person's name. Dozens of credit applications may be generated within a couple of weeks of a person's death. The debt goes to the deceased person's credit history, a special problem if a surviving person's credit is linked to that credit history.

AN EXAMPLE OF AN FTC CLARIFICATION

As stated earlier, the Federal Trade Commission is involved in the ongoing enforcement of the Funeral Rule. One example of a clarification of the Funeral Rule by the FTC was a ruling issued in July, 2005. The clarification helped to define the term "cash advance item" that appeared on some funeral homes' lists of goods and services (known officially at the FTC by the term "General Price List" — GPL). The FTC based this clarification on a review of the original Rule and the rulemaking record. The FTC found that the term "cash advance item" in the [Funeral] Rule "applies only to those items that the funeral provider represents expressly to be 'cash advance items' or represents by implication to be procured on behalf of a particular customer and provided to that customer at the same price the funeral provider paid for them."

THE NATIONAL FUNERAL DIRECTORS ASSOCIATION (NFDA) AND THE FUNERAL RULE

The National Funeral Directors Association (NFDA) is the major trade association to which funeral directors belong.

Here are two quotes regarding The Funeral Rule and NFDA's public policy positions from the editor of *The Director*, the official publication of NFDA, as published in *The Director* in May, 2007.

> "...this organization [NFDA] continues to fight the FTC Funeral Rule through its public policy positions."

And,

> "... it [NFDA] has also long had a Funeral Rule elimination policy on the books."

CALLING THE FTC

All funeral homes are very aware of the Funeral Rule. You may need to be firm with an individual funeral home about their obligation to follow the Funeral Rule. It will help to lower your funeral costs. If you run into problems, call the Federal Trade Commission at 1-877-FTC-HELP (1-877-382-4357); TTY: 1-866-653-4261.

REST *in* PEACE

5

30 IMPORTANT THINGS TO KNOW BEFORE YOU HIRE A FUNERAL DIRECTOR

Shop Around / Religious Preference / At the Funeral Home / Select a Funeral Director / No Magical Powers / Newspapers / You, the Funeral Director

SHOP AROUND

1. Shopping around for funeral services is a wise thing. Costs add up quickly, and, for a funeral, they frequently add up in hundreds and thousands of dollars at a time. Some funeral homes may not appear take you seriously in this effort. If they're smart they do. There are vendors ready to work with you. The AARP also recommends shopping around.

Religious Preference

2. Many funeral homes and directors have expertise with clients from certain religious backgrounds. If this is important to you, it's another reason to be in charge and plan in advance, so that you can have the religious ceremony and burial of your choice, while keeping costs down.

3. You have the right to your own religious preference, even if it is none. Your funeral is yours, and no one else's, whether you're Catholic, Protestant, agnostic, etc.

At the Funeral Home

4. A funeral home will consider you more seriously as a potential client when you ask for and read through their list of their goods and services. A list of goods and services is required by the government. (See the Funeral Bill of Rights in the previous chapter.) Remember, it is only a *statement* of goods and services. It is not a contract.

5. You do not have to accept a funeral package offered by a funeral home, ever. Packages may be constructed in such a way as to make shopping comparisons difficult. Persevere in asking enough questions to make apples-to-apples comparisons. If a funeral director won't give answers that

permit accurate comparisons, you may need to discard packages as potentially too costly. (As you might in a purchase from any other business.) You may also want to find a funeral director who can help you understand his information better, perhaps at a different funeral home.

SELECT A FUNERAL DIRECTOR

6. The funeral home will assign a funeral director to you. Even the services offered in the same funeral home may vary from director to director. *You do not have to accept the funeral director assigned to you.* Funeral directors have different skills and styles for creativity. Each funeral director has his own way of doing things. They talk differently from each other. They act differently from each other. They are different human beings. If you have been to several funerals you may have noticed this.

    How open and responsive does the funeral director seem to be, particularly to pricing questions? Choosing a funeral director you can talk to and negotiate with is important in lowering the cost. If you find that you can't talk, you can always walk on to the next funeral director or funeral home, before you sign a contract.

No Magical Powers

7. Funeral directors are not clergy. They do not have divine or magical powers with the dead. The amount of actual time a funeral director spends with the dead may be as low as one percent of time spent on the job.

8. Some funeral directors still offer services performed in the funeral home to "bless the dead" for a fee paid by the family. Be aware that this may represent a "blessing" that is not in keeping with your religious beliefs, traditions, and preferences. The word "blessing" in current language usage takes in a large amount of territory and many kinds of religions. So, if you desire to have this type of service, check with an ordained representative of your own religious community, especially someone you know.

9. Funeral home staff know that the memory of the deceased may have a lot of emotional power over you — anger, grief, guilt, etc. While appreciating the funeral home's good service, you need to keep in perspective your personal emotional vulnerability and the funeral home's business-oriented attention to it.

10. Funeral directors cultivate connections with clergy and churches throughout the community. This helps to build the funeral business finan-

cially, as well as keeping things running smoothly for individual funerals.

NEWSPAPERS

11. Most newspapers will not print an obituary that comes directly to them from anyone in the general public, including you or the next of kin. Newspapers will accept obituaries that are submitted to them by funeral directors. Part of this results from the need by newspapers for qualified, accurate reporting sources for one of the most important sections of the news that helps sell papers everywhere. The other part of the old financial link between funeral homes and newspapers that keeps the relationship bonded is that funeral homes advertise. If an individual complains to a newspaper about an obituary or a funeral, the newspaper may be more supportive of a funeral home.

12. NOTE: Because the following information related to obituaries and identity theft is important, it is repeated in a few places in this book, where obituaries are mentioned. WARNING: Whoever submits an obituary to a paper needs to protect both the living and dead from the identity theft that can start with an obituary. The AARP advises that no one should give a complete name or address for the deceased in an

obituary. Scammers may combine this information with other information purchased on the internet (including a social security number, etc.) and sell it as a package of information that helps other scammers open credit accounts, run up charges, purchase cars, ruin credit histories. This may include ruining the credit histories of living people linked to those accounts. Damage to credit may start to occur within a few weeks of publication of the obituary.

13. Embalming is not required for a viewing or a service. A family can request a **private viewing** with the funeral home. Most of the time, you'll want to keep a casket closed if you choose a burial without embalming. The condition of the deceased at the time of death, and the conditions under which the deceased is kept, affect whether the appearance of the deceased is suitable for any open casket display.

14. No one can put a time limit on the resolution of grief. Don't believe anyone, including a funeral director or member of the family, or clergy, who suggests to you that grief will be resolved by the time of the graveside service or through the purchase of any particular goods and services. Some grief may take months up to a couple of years to resolve. (But, grief doesn't need to define you or someone you care about or to

prevent you from walking forward and living the rest of your life.)

15. You can negotiate down the price of the casket. If you take care of other basics for the arrangements in advance, it will allow more time to negotiate the price of a casket when you need to, including the time to review prices at other vendors and the time to go to alternate sources and buy a casket, if casket negotiations with the funeral home you've chosen are not satisfactory.

16. Sealed caskets and vaults are not guaranteed to keep the elements out, no matter what a person selling them tells you.

17. While you can plan and carry out many of the things that a funeral director traditionally handles, you will need a funeral director to:

   ■ transport a deceased person.

   ■ sign a death certificate.

   ■ officially report the death to the Social Security Administration.

18. Local funeral societies and the Federal Trade Commission can assist you with the information you need to conduct a funeral service. Check for funeral societies in the Yellow Pages or on the internet. For the FTC, dial 1-877-FTC-HELP (1-877-382-4357); TTY: 1-866-653-4261.

19. Do not choose preneed. The AARP agrees. If funeral home staff try to sell you preneed for other family members or friends during the arrangement conference or the funeral service, immediately report the funeral home or the director to the FTC. You are unlikely to lower funeral costs talking with preneed salespeople, no matter when you speak with them.

20. If you are dealing with a funeral director who has the letters CPC (Certified Preneed Counselor) after his name, exercise caution. Preneed training has him focused on this area of sales for the funeral home.

21. If you are on public aid, you may qualify, in many states, to receive a full service funeral, including a public viewing, paid for by the government.

22. You can take as much time as you need or want and you can also leave or cancel an arrangement or prearrangement conference at any time during the conference. You can schedule to come back on a different day if need be.

23. In some states, people can train and qualify to become funeral insurance salespersons or prearrangers in three days to a week.

24. A good way to lower costs on your funeral is to pick up a casket near cost. This can be done on the internet or with the help of a funeral director.

He doesn't need to be working for a funeral home to obtain a casket. He just needs to be a licensed funeral director.

25. A rental casket may be rented *for the service only* in a funeral home or church. This is usually done when there will be a cremation. After the service, the deceased is transferred to the least expensive box for actual cremation. Sometimes if a deceased is cremated before a service, an urn may be placed inside a closed casket for the service.

26. Don't buy a Ziegler case for shipping your loved one. Check on purchasing an airtray, a much less expensive alternative.

27. Green funerals are very popular throughout the United Kingdom. There are plans for environmentally friendly funerals and cemeteries in the United States and Canada. The home funeral movement is also on the way.

28. At church or during the funeral service, someone can ask the minister to take an orchestrated offering for the family, in case of great financial need.

29. Another way potentially to lower the cost of a funeral is to consider donating your body to science. This must be arranged well in advance.

30. To eliminate the cost of a funeral home urn and a cemetery plot, and for the sake of complete portability, survivors can supply their own urn (needs

to be able to hold up to 10 pounds), and take the ashes with them.

Many funeral directors believe they are helping other people all the time, frequently thinking they are strong for others. You need to know that because you will be negotiating with them. You should not hand over control to them at any point in the process. It will not lower the cost of your funeral.

YOU, THE FUNERAL DIRECTOR

You, your designee, or next of kin is in charge of the funeral of you or your loved one, **not the funeral director**. This means that you are in charge, of the arrangement conference, the visitation, the funeral service, and the graveside service.

6

NEED PRENEED? KISS YOUR INTEREST(S) GOODBYE

Preneed Planning May Be Neither /
You Have No Interest in Preneed /
Preneed is Never Part of Aftercare

PRENEED PLANNING MAY BE NEITHER

People selling this product will tell you that you will lock in prices today and save money for the future.

Of course, that means that the funeral home will have your money and you will be hoping that they are in business when your need arrives. If anyone in a position with access to preneed funds decides to take the funds and go, there is usually no protection for you.

YOU HAVE NO INTEREST IN PRENEED

Preneed payments will add more long-term debt to your monthly living expenses. You do not receive interest.

Whether or not the company is in business when you die, and the preneed fund still exists, generally, you will never receive money back. Many things can happen in your life in the meantime. For example, you may move to a location that is not in the area covered by the funeral home. Preneed funds will waste money for a funeral. So, keep your money and the interest, and do not choose preneed.

If a preneed salesperson comes into your arrangement conference, get up, leave the premises, and call the Federal Trade Commission at 1-877-FTC-HELP (1-877-382-4357); TTY: 1-866-653-4261.

PRENEED IS NEVER PART OF AFTERCARE

Watch for preneed that is labeled as part of "Aftercare." Refuse to listen to anyone who wants to talk to you about planning for another funeral during an "aftercare" visit for a current funeral. Many funeral homes have no "aftercare." If they say they have an after service preneed program, but no aftercare, be very careful.

A classic line to open a preneed sales conversation is for a member of the funeral sales team to say, "I really care about you. Would you like to prearrange your funeral?" I have also heard a few preneed salespeople make a joking reference to the upcoming closing of a sale by saying, "I am going in for the kill."

Be aware that a funeral director with CPC (for Certified Preneed Counselor) after his or her name will be focused on preneed sales.

The AARP discusses preneed issues on its website.

CHAPTER 6

7

BE SURE YOU PREARRANGE THE ARRANGEMENTS

Prearranging / A Word About Selecting a Designee / Sites for the Visitation and Funeral Service / Doing What the Director Does / Items You Prearrange / A Word About Photos and Video-Slide Presentations / The Lowest Cost Procession

PREARRANGING

Prearranging in the normal context of a funeral home involves planning someone's funeral with them in advance. It's like a regular arrangement conference, but the death has not yet happened.

In this chapter, we're supplying a list of items that you can plan in advance that will be your own prearrangement of a funeral, with you serving as the funeral director. These are plans that you, or your designee, can later take into the arrangement conference with a licensed funeral director, that will lower the cost of a funeral.

Envision your funeral and script your vision for the visitation, funeral, and burial service, like the important person you are to your loved ones.

Whether you're wealthy or having a public aid funeral, whether the town will turn out or just a few friends will attend, you should plan. This is a final opportunity to express and bless others with the unique "you"they love.

Think about the great parts of life you've loved andthe people you've cared about. Think about the people who will be there. Think about the impact on them — and then plan.

A Word About Selecting a Designee

A designee steps in to complete the plan at the arrangement conference, after the loved one, who organized the plan, dies. The designee may also work alongside to help with the prearranging and will ultimately have the entire plan, in written form from you and prearranging information/materials with him/her before attending the arrangement conference.

Step 1: You need to designate someone to continue the role of the funeral director at your funeral (your next of kin or the executor of your estate is a good place to start). Read over the list in the chapter on the arrangement conference that follows this one and decide who can best serve as the designee.

Step 2: Remember, a licensed funeral director needs to be hired (probably at the arrangement conference) to care for the list of things that only a licensed funeral director is legally allowed to do, including:

- transporting your loved one to a funeral home

- embalming, or arranging for cremation

- leading an open road procession, if one is needed

- being present at the graveside, unless the family takes the ashes with them

- signing the death certificate

- notifying the Social Security Administration

You or a designee can handle the rest.

Step 3: Plan as though you are standing there next to your designee at the arrangement conference.

Step 4: Advise your designee to follow the *perfect 17 steps* outlined at the end of the next chapter in the section called, "*Scenes from a Perfect Arrangement.*"

Your designee needs to follow the plan and hold the funeral director to the Funeral Rule, to lower costs of the funeral.

ABOUT SITE SELECTION FOR THE VISITATION AND FUNERAL SERVICE

Planning starts with selecting the place. If you must be traditional, have the services at the funeral home, but expect to pay the price. To save money, it may be best not to use the funeral home.

A church, chapel, or even a community facility is fine. You could use a large yard or a park. You may choose to have a tent or not to have one. It is very easy to have the visitation and the funeral service at this type of alternate site. It could even be in your backyard. (A home funeral movement will be underway soon in this country.) Another good alternative is to have the funeral or memorial service at a nursing home where a loved one resided.

Selecting an alternate site is a strong tool for price reduction when working to reach a contract agreement for arrangements with a funeral director.

Doing What the Director Does —
Items You Can Prearrange to Lower
the Cost and Stress

1. *The Visitation*

Location, location, location. Find a site away from the funeral home to bring the cost down. An hour or two at the church prior to the funeral service makes sense.

2. *The Flowers*

Purchase discounted flowers on your own or buy flowers wholesale using your federal Tax Identification Number (TIN), if you have one. Have the flowers arranged separately for you. To save the stress of family disagreements, select someone to distribute flowers after the services.

3. *Memorial Folders*

Computers make this possible. Place a picture on the front and a poem inside with the dates of birth and death.

4. *Prayer Cards and Acknowledgement Cards*

Do these yourself. Order prayer cards from a wholesaler or make them. Place a picture on one side and a prayer on the other side with the dates of birth and death. An acknowledgement card helps people donate money to you, a charity, church, or non-profit cause. The card is usually in an envelope so that a donation can go inside.

5. **A Memorial Poster Board**

You can select pictures and place them on poster boards.

6. **Memorial CD and/or DVD**

A compact disc (CD) with music for the services and, perhaps, even the voice of the deceased and/or a DVD PowerPoint slideshow presentation with pictures and music. (See the section at the back of this chapter.) Save organist fees with a boombox.

7. **Register Book**

A guest book purchased at a discount store will work.

8. **Memorial Video**

An internet guide or your digital camera guide can show you how to do this.

9. **Memorial Website(s)**

Some are free. People are creating websites quickly these days. Funeral memorial websites can be placed on the web during the funeral time or longer. A fast way to do that is on www.MySpace.com where you get a website and a blog. Putting up a website is within everyone's reach now.

10. *The Eulogy*

Have someone write a eulogy, even if the minister delivers it. Some ministers have generic fill-in-the-blank eulogies that won't reflect the deceased. A eulogy is frequently memorable when delivered by a family member or friend.

11. *Cemetery Items*

Cemetery items including the plot, the vault, the liner, are not discussed in this book. The Funeral Consumers Alliance (FCA) addresses it well. I recommend that you contact them. They can send you a paperwork package that's a great asset in your planning (and is not preneed).

12. *The Funeral*

In the funeral plan you should include instructions for music, speakers, and the Order of Service.

13. *The Procession*

See the section at the end of this chapter for information.

14. *At the Graveside and for a Graveside Service*

If you want really to lower the cost, having just a graveside service may be a good way to go. You can do everything at the graveside that is done at the funeral home including the visitation, funeral service, memorial boards, the guest book, and the rest. You will need to plan to hire and pay the minister, the musician, the singers, the cemetery, the grave digger, and the vault man. You also will need to pay the vault company or the cemetery for a grave liner, if you decide not to have a fancy vault.

15. *The Gathering*

Plan your after-service dinner or gathering at home or at a restaurant. Some churches are able to provide kitchen and dining facilities. Other churches may have groups for hire that perform cooking and/or other serving functions as a means of fund raising for missions work they do.

16. *The Obituary*

Write the obituary ahead of time. Otherwise, the funeral director will interview you or the family designee for all the information to write the obituary, and it will add another service fee from the funeral home.

Open the obituary page of the newspaper in which you wish to place the obituary. Read several obituaries to become familiar with the style. Call the newspaper to double check their formatting preferences. To avoid identity theft, do not use the full name, address, or birth date of the deceased in the obituary.

While larger papers generally only receive obituaries submitted by funeral directors, it's worth calling to find out. If the newspaper tells you that the obituary must be submitted by the funeral director, remind them politely that you did most of the work.

In addition to posting an obituary in the newspaper, consider going to www.BlogSpot.com and posting it in a blog, for free.

17. *Dressing, Casketing, Cosmetics; Home Funerals*

You can also negotiate away charges for dressing, casketing, and cosmetics for your loved one, if you are willing to help. Yes, the family goes in to dress, apply cosmetics, and style the hair, or wig, of their loved one. Or, you may know a beautician who does this kind of work also and can style the hair and/or apply cosmetics for you. These may also be done as part of home-based funerals.

18. *Payment*

Leave instructions on how to pay for the funeral to save the stress of family disagreements.

51

19. *Religious Preference*

Leave instructions for your religious preference for services to save the stress of family disagreements.

20. *Clothing*

Select clothing for services/burial to save the stress of family disagreements.

21. *Caskets and urns*

Caskets are generally marked up 300 to 700 percent. Urns are marked up at the same rate.

For urns, decorative ceramic jars, glazed jars of any kind, or handmade urns, provided by a family member or yourself, can be more meaningful and less costly. The jar should be able to hold about ten pounds.

As stated in the Funeral Bill of Rights earlier, you have the right to get your casket or urn from another source other than the funeral home. If you go outside the funeral home for a casket or urn, you will save money, *not* have to sacrifice quality. Some people make their own caskets.

There is a growing alternative to cemeteries for the final burial site for an urn, called a columbarium. It's a very old idea that is reemerging. Usually a columbarium is a wall or structure built with niches in the walls to house urns. Even universities are building them to house old alumni who are interested in staying on campus. It may or may not be less expensive than a cemetery plot.

A Word About Photos and Video / Slide Presentations / DVD Memorials

Computers have expanded the ability to tell a person's life story with pictures during funeral and memorial services. This offers another area for the participation of individuals and families. Computer software, such as PowerPoint and similar graphics/picture-oriented programs, can be used to create great remembrance presentations and videos for display on large screens during services.

Many funeral homes offer this capability now. The work is most frequently outsourced to other companies on a rapid turnaround basis.

A family or individual can do the work easily at a low cost, if a computer, a scanner, and a program like PowerPoint (part of the Microsoft Office software) is on hand or available to them. More advanced and more costly software programs, such as Photoshop, offer extremely sophisticated abilities to retouch, repair and restore darkened, faded or torn photographs, including adding and removing individuals and groups from the scene and changing background scenery completely.

CHAPTER 7

Even the smallest churches now are able to run beautiful slideshow presentations with their equipment using your file on a disk.

Initiating an electronic "scrapbook" for each family member and loved one using PowerPoint or another program is a wonderful idea. Teens with computer skills, as well as their parents, or grandparents, can keep the electronic images and records in a format that is easily accessible when the opportunity comes to celebrate a life during a special birthday, anniversary or even during a funeral or memorial service. Add music to the file and colored frames with captions to the slides.

If a family has actual photographs that need to be scanned for such a presentation, the sooner the better. It's a great family night project that can be scheduled periodically for regular updates. What an excellent way to enhance the sense of family for all involved, and share computer wisdom at the same time.

If you're having a family reunion, ask someone to bring along a laptop computer and scanner and invite extended family members to bring photos that haven't been turned into computer files yet.

Traditional photographs, of course, also make excellent visual displays to place at the site of the visitation, funeral, or memorial observance in lieu of slideshows or videos.

Paper products (for example funeral programs and cards) as well as slideshow presentations are also as close as a website. Go to www.lowercostfunerals.com to see the full range of funeral services available when you click a mouse button.

THE LOWEST COST PROCESSION

Although exact laws vary from state to state, generally the funeral director must turn over a burial permit with the funeral director's signature to the cemetery at the time of the burial. Because of that, the funeral director is going to be at the cemetery whether he is involved in a car procession or not.

Some families eliminate the procession expense completely by telling the funeral director to meet them at the cemetery.

THE LOW COST PROCESSION

The procession of cars in a funeral is a show of honor and respect for a loved one and the family made by all the people who accompany the body on the journey to its final resting place. As with other parts of the funeral process, funeral directors may say that this needs to be left to the professionals (that is, the funeral directors).

CREATING THE LIST, DETERMINING THE ORDER

To create a funeral procession, a funeral director starts by filling out a car list (the order of the funeral procession). He gets all the information from you. It's best, then, to fill out the car list before the arrangement conference.

The first car on the list usually is for members of the immediate family: wife, husband, father, mother, son, daughter, etc. The relationship of the next of kin is used to determine the rest of the order in the procession. It is usually the family, including cousins, and close friends, who follow in the car immediately behind the hearse. The order is generally on a first-come basis.

If you have a car list ahead of time, you can eliminate (through negotiation) some of the hourly fees for these vehicle services including the list creation and actual parking.

WHO'S PARKING AND DIRECTING THE CARS?

At some point in the past when you've driven by a funeral home, you may have seen people parking the cars. You may be surprised to learn that many times a funeral director is parking the cars. A funeral director is usually paid something over $22.00 per hour to do this. Do you need a valet who is paid over $22.00 per hour to park the cars for your funeral? It's more cost effective to have friends of the family direct the cars to the order of the car list, when forming a procession, or to open parking areas.

I have seen this a few times and can recommend it. Tell the funeral director that your family and friends will direct the traffic. Funeral directors are not traffic police. Most families have some members or friends who are able to do this.

Another option for cost savings is to have family members participate with only one funeral director involved in the process, rather than paying two or more funeral directors to direct parking.

Something I have seen several times is friends of the family passing out funeral stickers for the procession after a funeral service. This adds a point of personal connection for members of the procession.

You can also run your procession from the cemetery gates. If the cemetery is in a rural or uncongested area with plenty of parking, you may want to have people walk from the entrance.

Frequently, a funeral home owner may insist thatit's necessary to have a lead car for the funeral director and clergy that goes ahead of the hearse. This isn't needed.It's more cost efficient for the family if the clergy rides with a family member. It can also be a great help forthe family.

Leave the Open Road to the Professionals

Funeral directors are right about leaving an open road procession to them (that is, on busy city streets, highways, or anywhere outside the funeral home-church-burial site). Funeral processions on the open road are hazardous. If at all possible, make sure you have a police escort. A police escort provides safety and peace of mind for the family and everyone in the procession.

And finally worth noting, a pallbearer car traditionally is provided by the funeral home. Instead, simply have the pallbearers ride in one of their own cars. If you wish to have the pallbearers in a fancy car, rent one yourself.

8

NOT UNTIL IT'S OVER:
PAY AT THE END

Paying at the End /Paying Through Insurance / Pay-By Dates

PAYING AT THE END

Some funeral homes and funeral directors require that you pay in full as early as the arrangement conference. Some even will require payment before a contract is signed! You will never be able to lower the cost of your funeral if you pay for it all in advance. When you put a roof on your house, do you pay the full price to the contractor before the work is complete?

If the funeral home suddenly becomes very busy with several other client funerals during the time when your services are scheduled, and you have paid in advance, you lose your ability to leverage for any additional needs that occur. You want to receive the funeral home's best attention to performance and service for the work covered by your contract.

Overall, a funeral is a subjective experience. It's not unlike a flower arrangement you order for someone over the phone. The moment you order and pay for the flowers, it's completely in the hands of the florist as to how the bouquet will look, how many flowers they will use, or what they think may be substituted in the flower arrangement to make up for a lack of some kinds of flowers in the shop at the time. This could especially be true if a florist were to become busy with many or large orders at once.

It's difficult to evaluate results for some of the funeral services performed. Every person will have a different opinion. For this reason alone, it is best to wait to pay until the services are complete. If you pay ahead of time you are giving over control of the subjective experience to the funeral home and the funeral directors.

In my opinion, if you wait to pay for the funeral until the end, the funeral director remains responsive to you and you will continue to have greater input in the process.

PAYMENT THROUGH INSURANCE?

Funeral homes have a form for you to fill out that allows you to sign over your loved one's life insurance policy to make the funeral home or funeral director the first beneficiary on the policy. Don't do this. It will not help you lower the cost of the funeral.

Pay-By Date?

Another way funeral homes seek to control terms of payment is to have you sign up for a specific "pay-by" date. Don't sign off on a date that comes before the funeral ends. Consider very carefully the date when you can afford to make payment. A funeral home can use this date to take you to court — and have you pay their lawyer fees — if you fail to pay on time, by the date specified. You usually won't go to court, but usually you *will* pay for the funeral plus the funeral home's lawyer fees.

CHAPTER 8

9

THE ARRANGEMENT CONFERENCE: A MEETING OF THE MINDS WITH YOUR HAND ON YOUR WALLET

Prepare Your People / When You Discuss Arrangements Who is Speaking for the Funeral Home? / The Opening Pitch / Scenes from a Perfect Arrangement / Additional Thoughts

PREPARE YOUR PEOPLE

No one should attend an arrangement conference alone. It is beneficial to take along a trusted, knowledgeable friend(s) and/or family member(s) who is good with business details to make notes on the discussions, especially the pricing.

63

If you're a designee, this is the time for which you prepared. Another key to lower funeral costs is to have the people with you prepared for the arrangement conference. Let them know what they can expect (after you've read this chapter). They need to know that you have the right to take as long as you want to make the arrangements. You have the right to leave and come back to finish the conference (not just for a trip to the restroom).

Take a list with you that details your rights in purchasing funeral goods and services. Assemble and take along all the prearrangement materials, and a full written plan that includes all the instructions. If you/your designee has read and followed through on suggestions in the last chapter about the prearrangement of the funeral, you're in a good place to work through negotiations and the contract at the arrangement conference.

WHEN YOU DISCUSS ARRANGEMENTS WITH THE FUNERAL DIRECTOR, WHO IS SPEAKING FOR THE FUNERAL HOME?

At the opening of the arrangement conference you will probably be speaking to the funeral director. Asnegotiations get underway for the final contract for goods and services, the funeral director may bring in the manager or owner of the funeral home. This happens in somewhat the same way that a sales manager approves or finishes the negotiations for a car salesman.

Keep in mind that funeral arrangements are a $3,000 to $10,000 contract negotiation. A funeral director is paid to schedule and contract for a $10,000 dollar funeral in a couple of hours. (Perhaps you spent more time researching a car you wanted to buy that cost that much.) When you bought a car you eventually negotiated with the man with the big desk in the big office.

Whether you're speaking with the funeral director or the funeral home owner/manager, always be respectful, kind, and firm at the same time. You may need to come back to meet with the owner/manager, if you think doing that will move the contract discussions forward and he isn't there.

THE OPENING PITCH

The first thing the funeral director is likely to say is: "We will get this done in several hours." Like any salesman, what he says and does throughout the arrangement conference is preplanned. Because of the need to put potential clients at ease and to express genuine sympathy for the loss, the funeral director's demeanor is more subdued than that of salespeople in some other businesses. The funeral director will ask the designee and other survivors to talk about their loved one.

Let's take a step-by-step look at the arrangement conference.

SCENES FROM A PERFECT ARRANGEMENT — THE PERFECT 17 FOR THE ARRANGEMENT CONFERENCE

1. The designee(s) (see the chapter, *Be Sure You Prearrange the Arrangements*) and other survivors are well acquainted with the plan of their loved one, because it was made and shared in advance with the people who would be attending the arrangement conference. The designee(s) was briefed in detail and has all the materials necessary, including written plans, to bring to the arrangement conference. The rest of the survivors are aware of the basics of the plan.

2. The designee walks into the arrangement conference room with three bags.

3. The funeral director begins the arrangement conference by asking the designee and other survivors to talk about their loved one.

4. At the conclusion of the discussion, or when appropriate, the designee mentions that the loved one organized the details over a period of time and brings out the three bags.

5.   The first bag has visitation mementos and the memorial DVD, previously prepared. The bag also includes the plans and materials for the memorial folders, prayer cards, register book, and even a large photo to go above the register stand. (Because the memorial folders and prayer cards need a date of death inserted, the job hasn't been completed, but will be delivered in time for the funeral.)

6.   The second bag has the family's service notes and contacts (church or other site information), including the Order of Service, service instructions, singer and organist instructions, cemetery instructions, instructions for the grave digging, and vault instructions. It also contains the full obituary and eulogy instructions. (The obituary does not list anyone's full name, address, or birth date, to save everyone the problems of identity theft.)

7.   The third bag has clothing that was preselected by the loved one, necessary for display, embalming, or cremation. (This decision in advance by the loved one removes the possibility of a family disagreement on the matter.)

8.   The designee mentions that the loved one selected the flowers, and that the flowers will probably be purchased separately and delivered to the sites.

9. The designee has checked the minister's schedule and advises the funeral director of the location and date and time of the visitation, funeral, and/or graveside services that will be needed.

10. The family members bring up their decision to have gifts sent to (blank) charity in lieu of flowers. If there had been a financial hardship, especially as a result of the death, they would have requested that gifts be sent to: the designee's address, made out to (blank), in care of the family of (blank). But since the family is much better off than so many who need help, and their loved one had designated a charity to which gifts should be directed, this request can be honored.

11. There should be an arrangement for the return of any jewelry that was on the deceased immediately after the casket is closed.

12. The designee negotiates the price of the few remaining items, leaving the casket for last. The negotiations are much less stressful, because there are many less items on the agenda.

13. The survivors and designee have asked for and received a casket price list. This lets them know the prices of less expensive caskets, so that they are not shown only more expensive caskets by the funeral home staff. The funeral home is obligated by law to supply this price list.

14. The designee needs to tell the funeral director to allow time in the schedule at the graveside (if there is a burial) for the family to receive condolences face-to-face there from people who attend. If the family has chosen to cover the casket at the end of the funeral with flowers or dirt, the funeral director needs to allow time for that also.

15. As final negotiations for the contract for goods and services approaches, the funeral director may bring in the manager or owner of the funeral home.

16. The designee negotiates a price on a casket/urn, knowing that if the price remains too high, the casket/urn can be searched out on internet. Because of the Funeral Rule, the casket or urn can purchased from another company and used in the funeral home.

17. Based on the negotiations, a contract is issued by the funeral director that contains only the goods and services approved by the designee and the prices that were negotiated. The contract is read over by at least two or three of the group attending the conference. The survivors and designee have completed their loved one's plan for a lower cost funeral and leave together to go to lunch or dinner.

CHAPTER 9

ADDITIONAL THOUGHTS

Funeral home personnel will be focused on their ability to provide you with their full slate of services. You need to remember *your rights* as you negotiate prior to receiving the contract at the funeral home. So, negotiate away, until you reach a "meeting of the minds," that is, the basis of a contract that you will be satisfied with, that you can sign.

Again, a copy of the funeral home's contract should be carefully read through by at least two people before anything is signed. Above all, you are not under any obligation to sign any document the funeral home presents to you at any time. If items appear in the contract that you do not want included, strike them out.

As you negotiate and at the point of reading over thecontract, before you sign, be sure to stay together with friends and family. Be aware that some funeral home staff may distract friends and family from key points of negotiations and the signing of the contract through engaging them in other conversations at these critical times. This may even happen if the person who comes with you is a clergyperson. The distracting influence by the funeral staff is used to isolate the person taking financial responsibility for the funeral, the one who will be signing the contract. I hope that you won't be negotiating with anyone who conducts business that way in any industry.

Be sure to get a copy of the contract, immediately after you sign it.

CHAPTER 9

10

A SALUTE TO VETERANS: THE COUNTRY REMEMBERS YOUR SERVICE

An Ultimate Tribute / Spouses and Dependent Children of Qualified Veterans

AN ULTIMATE TRIBUTE

Today in the United States, veterans of wartime are invited to have their funerals and burials in one of the national cemeteries. The U.S. government provides a fitting memorial for those have given military service to our country. Normally a discharge paper is required.

At a national cemetery there are no charges for:

- A grave opening
- A grave closing
- A vault or liner
- The setting of a marker.

73

Please go to www.cem.va.gov for more information.

SPOUSES OF QUALIFIED VETERANS

Spouses of qualified veterans are entitled to a lot and marker in a national cemetery. Call 1-800-827-1000 to contact a Veterans office in your area that can help.

If your loved one was an eligible veteran, but was not buried in a national cemetery, call 1-800-827-1000 to obtain a burial allowance that will help pay the cost of theburial you did have.

REST *in* PEACE

PART III

Funeral Cost Flashpoints

11

FINANCIAL FLASHPOINTS

Flashpoints / To Avoid Financial Flashpoints / Will or Living Trust / Credit Cards / IRS / Insurance Policies / Veterans / Doing the Work

FLASHPOINTS

In firefighting, a flashpoint occurs when everything combustible at a fire scene — in a room, a house, a manufacturing facility, a forest — spontaneously bursts into flame all at once, vastly increasing the size of the fire and the speed with which it spreads. After the flashpoint is reached, it can be extremely difficult to fight a fire.

A death can set off flashpoints for the living. Two possible types of flashpoints proceeding from a death are financial and relationship flashpoints. (See the next chapter also.)

To Avoid Financial Flashpoints

Pay or be sure payment is made on the following for the deceased person (and keep records):

- current bills

- any known debts

- rent or mortgage and insurance policies on property

- any outstanding real estate taxes

As a family member or next of kin, be sure to follow the wishes of the deceased on all financial matters. To do anything else will not stand up in court if there is a challenge. This is important if you are temporarily caring for property of the deceased, but you are not the named executor of the estate.

Additional Financial Items to Complete

Will or Living Trust

Write a will or set up a living trust while you are alive. This will keep your assets from having to go through probate court — a big expense that cuts into your estate.

Credit Cards

Check on the status of credit card accounts, especially for joint accounts. Cancel or change names on credit cards or close accounts, as appropriate. This can escalate to trouble quickly, if you don't. Before you take action, be sure to understand how your credit may be affected by this death if you are linked on an account. It is usually best to call the credit card companies.

IRS

I'm sorry to mention this, but do call the Internal Revenue Service. Make an accurate list of "last illness" expenses and burial expenses for use with the IRS tax form 1040-706. Call or visit a local IRS office. They're very understanding about death. They may not be as understanding about taxes that aren't paid.

Social Security

Mail back or pay back any Social Security checks made to the deceased after death. The IRS and Social Securitywill track checks and dates against the death certificate. A funeral director is required to send a certified death certificate to the Social Security Administration. Penalties may be charged if the law has been violated. It is best to call or visit the local Social Security office.

Insurance Policies

Be sure that you receive all insurance policy funds that are owed to you. Be ready to provide death certificates for any insurance company where there was a policy. If you have the name of the local insurance agent for the deceased's policies, call the agent. He or she can call the national office of the insurance company and start the process moving. Be sure to call the national office yourself as well. You will need to have proper forms sent to you, NOT to your funeral director or lawyer. If you don't have the policies, call the policy search division of the American Council of Life Insurance at1-202-624-2000.

Obtaining Copies of the Death Certificate

Here's another tip to lowering the cost of a funeral. Between 10 and 20 certified copies of the death certificate may be needed to complete all transactions to do with banks, auto titles, property titles, etc., after a death. If the deceased had no assets, only one or two certified copies of the death certificates will be needed.

If you go to the funeral home for this service, the funeral home will list this death certificate fee with other administrative (paperwork) fees as part of "basic service for funeral director and staff" in "aftercare." (Sometimes the ONLY service performed by a funeral home as "aftercare" is dropping off the death certificate at the house of the next of kin.) The price given on a funeral home's list of goods and services for this "aftercare" will be inflated. Negotiate down the price. Always be sure to ask what is meant by "administrative services" and "aftercare," and exactly what they include. If the funeral home gives you a problem with this, get one certified copy of the death certificate through them and get the rest you need yourself.

A death certificate requires signatures of both a doctor and the funeral director. Usually, you can ask the funeral director to drop off at the County Health Department the death certificate that was signed by the doctor and the funeral director. Then the next of kin can pick up copies of the certified death certificate from the County Health Department. The fee for this will be the county's fee only.

Don't let the funeral home suggest a lawyer for this — to help you obtain what is easily obtained through your County Health Department. You will just add legal costs to an inflated funeral home fee. Handle as much as you can of the death certificate process on your own.

Veterans

If your loved one was an eligible veteran, but was not buried in a national cemetery, call 1-800-827-1000 to obtain a burial allowance that will help pay the cost of theburial you did have.

Doing the Work

Most funeral directors will say, "I'm not a lawyer" and will **advise you to have a lawyer complete items**

with legal ramifications, including some of the ones listed above. Funeral directors will often suggest that they can work with your lawyer. Be sure to do as many of the items listed above (and other common sense things) as you can on your own. The less work the funeral director and a lawyer have to do, of course, the less it will cost you.

12

RELATIONSHIP FLASHPOINTS

Grief, Mourning, Bereavement /
Responses to a Person Who Has Grief /
The Road Best Traveled

RELATIONSHIP FLASHPOINTS

One death may break apart an old family system, whether functional or dysfunctional. The roles of individual family members change in uncomfortable surroundings, testing the depth of relationships while, perhaps, establishing new patterns for decision-making.

A person nearing the end of emotional resources in this situation needs to call for help:

- ■ a pastor, priest, minister, chaplain or other clergy,

- ■ closest family members,

- ■ closest friend,

- the funeral director (careful here), if the director has been selected and the matter relates to the funeral home's participation in the funeral.

Additionally, the person should:

- Designate someone else to answer the phone and door.

- Ask another person to contact those hard-to-get-hold-of people who must know.

- Appoint someone to help care for gathering funeral information and obtaining pricing (as necessary), coordinating and attending arrangement conferences and making and completing plans.

- Appoint someone who is less emotionally connected to the deceased to be communicator for the family.

Remember the old Tommy Smothers line about his brother, "Mom always liked you best?" Conflicts that existed in life may not die with the death of you or a loved one.

If you have the opportunity, it is a great gift to someone else to take the lead, while you are alive, to resolve these issues. Even the simple act of planning a funeral in advance can start a dialog. You may not have partnered with another person for a long time to plan anything else in life. Planning your own funeral certainly calls for relying on other people.

GRIEF, MOURNING, BEREAVEMENT

Grief is the state of emotion that follows a loss. Mourning is the outward expression of that emotion. Bereavement usually refers to the loss through death of a beloved person.

One of the less recognized casualties of scientific and social changes during the last century may be the mourning and grieving process. Once death has been certified and the body removed, family and friends have very little contact with the deceased. The visitation and/or wake take place, followed by the funeral service and burial. In the words of one minister:

> "The customs and structure which gave recognition to mourning [the outward expression of the emotion of grief] a hundred years ago barely exist today. While there are many books and studies on grief, once the funeral is over, survivors are generally expected to pull themselves up by their bootstraps, swallow their pain, and resume life as before. There has been a shift in cultural viewpoint from expressing mourning as an integral and important part of grief,

to one where the pain of bereavement must be concealed."

Modern life doesn't allow a lot of room for the many months, up to a couple of years, that an individual may require to process grief.

Of course, the grieving process can be detoured at any point, by anyone, after the death of a loved one has occurred. A hospital ER observer witnessed this:

> A woman and her friend rushed into the emergency room where the woman's husband had been brought, quite likely already dead. Another friend of the couple arrived shortly, the leader of a large Sunday school class at her church. ER efforts at resuscitation went on for some time. Finally, a doctor announced the husband's time of death.
>
> The Sunday school friend assured the newly bereaved wife that she could take comfort that her husband was now in a better place — and prayerfully gave thanks. The wife, struck silent, nodded her head. In a few minutes, the Sunday friend left for an unbreakable appointment, promising to call.

The second friend, who had been standing with the wife, said "Even though you know he's in heaven, it's hard to let him go isn't it?" The tears the wife had held back burst out, and she wept for several minutes, holding her husband's hand and stroking his face.

Spiritual truth, even if accurate and well-intentioned, may need to be reserved for a moment when it can provide its true consolation for a person currently experiencing grief. A person in grief right now, may need only to have their story heard, right now, or to spill stored tears, right now, to a listener who is sensitive to the pain of the moment.

DO NOT SAY THE FOLLOWING TO A GRIEVING PERSON

- I know just how you feel.

- It was God's will.

- God needed another rose in his garden (nothing overly sentimental).

- He's in a better place.

- You're young; you can or will remarry.

- You can always have another child.

- It was only an infant, you never knew her.

- It's time to get over it and move on.

BETTER RESPONSES TO A GRIEVING PERSON

- I am so sorry for your loss.

- Let me know how I can help you with the funeral.

- Could I have your permission to help direct traffic?

- I'd like to bring you a meal tonight; can I do that?

  (*Watch out regarding the food. There could be too much. If you're in a church setting, it would be good to set up a schedule of meals with other people. Coordinate care for other needs.*)

- Shared silence (as appropriate)

- Quiet listening

- Companionship

Don't just do nothing, because you don't know what to do. Do something to acknowledge the loss — make a phone call or send a card — and do it as soon as possible.

Some funeral home websites now include an address to which to send e-mails of sympathy to survivors.

Do not avoid the person who has suffered the loss just because you don't know what to say. If your friendship was based on going out together as couples, make sure that you're including the grieving spouse in your invitations and your conversations, as before. One widow remarked to a grief support group about how isolated she felt just sitting in the back seat of another couple's car without her husband. The couple was together and she felt, and was, by herself, even in their company. You can't fix everything for someone else, but you can be sensitive to their pain.

Unfortunately, within a few weeks after a loss, the community and world around a survivor may move on while the life of the one who has suffered the loss has changed in a more permanent way, with pain over the loss continuing.

A survivor may need social and emotional support from three months up to two years or more, after the loss. Some people have found that the second year after the loss was harder than the first.

Offering practical assistance that leads to shared times of friendship helps build up the survivor in just living normal aspects of everyday life and moving forward. Don't overdo it, making the person dependent on you. Be helpful, without being over-bearing. You're not there to be a permanent rescuer, but to walk along with them for a while.

Sometimes grieving people develop physical illnesses or symptoms as a result of grief. If you are a friend of a survivor, who mentions that he or she is having trouble with sleeping, eating, or other physical problems, gently ask if he or she has seen a doctor, and if not, suggest it.

Be aware that anniversary dates, especially during the first year, may be difficult. Call and say, "I'm thinking of you," "wonder how you're doing," "what are your plans for that day" (on the birthday of the person who died or the survivor's own birthday). Possibly plan an activity.

THE ROAD BEST TRAVELED

A person experiencing loss through death, after two to three months, sometimes sooner, may be open to getting support in a group setting at a grief support group.

If you don't know of a grief support group, check for one at local hospitals, hospices, or churches.

Assure your friend that there is nothing to be lost and much to be gained by seeing a professional counselor with counseling credentials, social worker, psychologist or psychiatrist skilled in recovery from grief.

A therapist may gently urge a person into the realization that he or she can move on.

GRIEF SUPPORT SERVICES, GRIEF COUNSELING, AND "AFTERCARE"

Funeral home packages may include items labeled "grief support services" or "grief counselor" separately or as a part of "aftercare." There is a wide range of counseling qualifications represented in these labels that should be checked out before purchase. Funeral homes may not be the most appropriate places to find counseling and support services for dealing with the grief that comes from the loss of a loved one.

CHAPTER 12

PART IV

How-To: Examples of Low Cost, No Cost (!?!) Less Stress Funerals

13

THE LOW COST, LESS STRESS TIES THAT BIND

A Great and Joyful Noise / The Procession and the Covering

A GREAT AND JOYFUL NOISE

One of the most jubilant funerals I have seen was for a woman who died with no money, but who was rich with friends. It was one of the most pure definitions of a low cost, less stress funeral.

The woman's church printed the memorial folders and prayer cards along with the Order of Service programs at the church and brought them to the funeral home.

The body was in a closed casket and did not require embalming.

When the family came to the funeral home for the service, they brought the entire church with them. The choir came, the assistant pastor came, the ushers came, the congregation came. There was a great and joyful noise that rocked the funeral home on its foundation that day. The church took an offering at the funeral service.

THE PROCESSION AND THE COVERING

It was quite a large funeral, with a dramatic procession to the cemetery — police escort and all. When we arrived at the cemetery, almost out of nowhere 500 people assembled at the gravesite. Arriving at the cemetery, the minister requested that everyone stay for the closing of the grave. The minister's eulogy was eloquent.

The casket was lowered into the ground. The minister took a shovel and symbolically placed dirt on the grave. Members of the congregation waited in line to take handfuls of dirt and toss them on the casket. A backhoe then filled in the grave.

Several people in the congregation took off their hats, all kinds of hats. Throughout the congregation, people took a few dollars out of their pockets. The hats were passed through the large crowd and filled with an offering for the family. The collection at the graveside that day more than paid for the funeral.

To the funeral director's amazement, people came up and thanked him. Many people said that it felt so good to place the dirt on the grave. Others came up and said that it felt good to see dirt covering the grave.

From dust we come and to dust we go.

CHAPTER 13

14

THE WOMAN AND THE CASKET

*The Son / The Husband /
A Special Gift / The Wife*

THE SON

The son — a handful while growing up, rebellious by his own admission — first saw the birch, plywood casket embellished with a carved cross, while on business in another state. Matching caskets were purchased for his mother and father.

THE HUSBAND

His father, speaking some time later at the funeral of his wife of 64 years, told the public assembly looking at the lovely, varnished, plain wood, that his wife, "…was an incredible woman; I wish you could look in her casket, because she is so beautiful. I sat there a long time last night looking at her…."

A Special Gift

The man who took the order from the son, had started the casket-making business in the place where he resided in Louisiana, using his special gift to help bury fellow residents who couldn't afford caskets. The casket cost $215. Unusually, for a casket, the names of the three men who made it were burned into the side.

The men who made the casket were all prisoners at the Louisiana State Penitentiary. The prisoner who had started the program was buried in one of his own caskets, 31 years into serving his sentence at the prison, several months before the completion of what he considered his proudest achievement.

The Wife

The prisoner's proudest achievement held the remains of another gift: a fun-loving, creative, intelligent wife, mother, grandmother, author, Sunday school teacher, who was born in China and had had dreams of returning to Tibet as a missionary, until she met a young man at the Illinois college they both attended. The casket made of plywood at the prison, purchased by their son, Franklin, held the body of Ruth Graham, the wife of Billy Graham.

15

A CHURCH AT THE COUNTRY CEMETERY

A Gift of Strength / I Saw the Light

A GIFT OF STRENGTH

Another beautiful, memorable, very low cost funeral took place completely at a small country cemetery.

The whole church came to the cemetery. One man held the register book for people to sign. The minister arrived early with a large speaker system that was then wired from his car to the gravesite. Another member of the congregation, a gravedigger, had dug the grave in advance. (Those gifted with physical strength among friends can offer this to a family experiencing loss.)

The body had been cremated (saving embalming/casket costs). The family provided their own urn. The cemetery did not require an urn vault (saving $400 to $600).

I Saw the Light

A woman handed out memorial folders that had been created by church members. When all the folders were distributed, the congregation began by singing "Praise the Lord, I Saw the Light." (Find the Johnny Cash version if the tune doesn't immediately pop to mind. It's a classic.) Several more songs followed.

The minister gave a powerful homily and eulogy. After more songs, the assembly finished with, "Ain't No Grave Gonna Keep This Body Down." The funeral director was completely awestruck — with the rest of the people.

16

JUST IMAGINE

Shared Remembrance / A Private Memorial / Under the Palm Trees at the Funeral Home / Caring Friends / I Can Only Imagine

SHARED REMEMBRANCE

The Iraq conflict is changing the face of some funeral services. I've had the privilege of working with families who have lost loved ones in Iraq. One particular family had a loved one who was working there as a civilian when he was killed by terrorists at a major installation.

The family was having a very hard time with the loss, of course. They could not agree on a moderator for the service. Tension rose as the discussion went back and forth for quite a while about the service and how best to memorialize their loved one. I was concerned for them. The funeral was to be high profile, with some higher level military personnel coming in from Iraq. Expressing regret, I finally had to let the family know that they needed to come to some decisions. I could make decisions for them or they could do just about everything themselves.

We discussed the family's options of having a formal service or a sharing service, where people stand up and share stories and anecdotes of life with the deceased. They could select any moderator, minister, or friend of their choosing to preside over the service. We discussed what the minimum number would be for the Order of Service programs and memorial cards.

I told them that I was going to step away from the arrangement conference so they could decide what they were going to do. Later, to my surprise, the family asked me to be the moderator and to write the Order of Service. The family chose to have their own memorial cards printed. They went to a neighborhood instant print shop.

The sharing format for the funeral service that the family selected was a deeply effective way to tell the loved one's life story from childhood through tours of duty in Iraq, by using the stories from many friends and family members who attended the service. In doing so, the family created a funeral that was itself a warm and positive time of remembrance for everyone who attended, sealing forever in the hearts of many people what that vibrant life had meant. The funeral director did not make a large profit for the the funeral home corporation he worked for at the time.

NOTE: when using an open sharing service, have two or three planned speakers to call on to start the sharing time.

It's important that whoever moderates the sharing time thanks each person who speaks, immediately after they have shared. No matter how emotional the speech was, thank them. It affirms the speaker in the gift of love that was just made.

Also, be sure that everyone participates who wishes to, as they are able. For example, a child might read a poem or light a memorial candle.

A Private Memorial

Another deeply affecting funeral where the family chose to do much of the work, and paid less, was one for a young, disabled girl. This child knew that she was going to die, so she made her own memorial folders and Order of Service. The family took care of their own music as well.

They used a funeral home for the services, but gave the instruction that funeral directors should not be involved. They used an open sharing format for the services.

While the family could easily have negotiated discounted services, they did not to do that.

Under the Palm Trees at the Funeral Home

A colorful funeral, that focused on the joy of life, was planned by a man who loved his wife dearly. He also loved vacations in Hawaii.

He decked out the entire funeral home with their collected Hawaiian memorabilia. It was like being on the beach on Oahu. There were Hawaiian dancers.

In terms of the funeral home, all this man did was to have a direct cremation and rent three rooms in the funeral home for three days. It was a good funeral at a lower cost.

Caring Friends

Another memorable funeral took place entirely at the cemetery. The woman did not have much interaction with her children. Her death was sudden.

It was not an extremely large crowd, but it was a caring one. There was a closed casket, with embalming.

Because it was a public aid funeral, it did not cost much. The full visitation, funeral, and burial were held at the graveside. Everyone was kind to the family, and they did not incur heavy expenses.

I Can Only Imagine

A final funeral I would like to mention was a simple direct burial. There was no minister. A family member made a few comments. The family had a boom box and played I Can Only Imagine by Mercy Me. People listened and cried at this gravesite and also at two other adjacent funerals.

CONCLUSION

DUST TO DUST

Let us know how to measure our days and what is valuable while we are here.

THE THREE MORTAL FACTS OF IT ALL

1. The first reality is that death happens — to everyone. According to author Jane Walmsley: "the single thing to know about Americans is [that] they think...death is optional." It is coming to you whether you deny it or not.

2. The second reality is that a day above ground is important for you and for the people left behind here. You have one life. Saving on a funeral and investing in what brings life is important. Spend the savings on a worthwhile charity, your family, yourself. Seriously, about charity, what if $1000, $3000, or more doesn't go into the ground for eternity in the form of a more expensive casket, etc., but instead goes to dig a few wells around the world for a few villages out of the thousands that could use help? Or maybe you know someone in your family or the neighborhood who could use assistance paying the rent or paying a bill. There is no reason not to lower the cost of your funeral, or to put more money than necessary into the ground.

3. The third mortal reality is that you should plan ahead for the day below ground. It is easier than ever to plan effectively, using your computer and the internet. Having a plan and executing the plan is a key to life — and death.

In *Rest In Peace*, we have discussed key elements of planning that will help you to lower the cost of a funeral and should result in savings of at least $1,000 on a $6,000 funeral (and more than that in some cases, depending on funeral type and locality).

We've explored strategies to help you lessen the stress of a funeral for you and your loved ones.

We've reviewed powerful tools to prepare you for the Arrangement Conference, while lowering the costs and stress.

Taking advantage of lower costs and a detailed plan can lead to fewer family disagreements about how to honor a loved one and how to spend money on a funeral.

Planning ahead can create a place for each member of your family during the funeral process and give each person highly valued memories. Planning ahead gives greater peace of mind to the friends and surviving members of your family. This helps your family to move forward in a unified way for a special time of reflection and remembrance.

While the greatest benefits will occur if you plan in advance, *Rest in Peace: Insider's Tips to The Low Cost, Less Stress Funeral* will help in whatever funeral situation you find yourself. It can be a fast reference on funerals or an advance planning opportunity to create a funeral at a lower cost with less stress.

Do you need more information?

The author is only a mouse click or a phone call away. Visit:

www.LowerCostFuneral.com

Change is not merely necessary to life, it is life.

~ Alvin Toffler

ABOUT THE AUTHOR

The author, R. Brian Burkhardt is licensed as a funeral director in Illinois and Virginia. He has worked for several funeral homes in both states and has arranged many funeral services at Arlington National Cemetery. Prior to becoming a funeral director, R. Brian Burkhardt was a certified manager with a national newspaper chain.

Most recently, R. Brian started his own company and does consulting work on every aspect of funerals. His main website is **www.RBrianBurkhardt.com**.

R. Brian holds a degree in Political Science from Illinois State University and also has a degree in Mortuary Science. He resides in the Chicago area, with his wife and two children. R. Brian's experiences in the funeral industry have prompted him to write this book.

RESULTS

FROM THE USE OF THIS BOOK WILL VARY DEPENDING ON NEGOTIATIONS AND THE PARTIES INVOLVED

LEGAL NOTICE

All users are advised to retain competent counsel, if it becomes necessary to determine what state or local funeral laws or regulations may apply to the user's particular situation.

The purchaser or reader of this publication assumes responsibility for the use of these materials and information.

Adherence to all applicable laws and regulations, federal, state, and local, governing professional licensing and contract negotiating, and Funeral Law and other aspects of doing business in the United States or any other jurisdiction is the sole responsibility of the purchaser or the reader.

The author, the editor/writer, and the publisher assume no responsibility or liability whatsoever on behalf of any purchaser or reader of these materials.

Any perceived slights of specific people or specific organizations are unintentional.

HELPFUL LINKS

Hospitals have their patient advocates. Who will be your funeral advocate? I am sure of one thing: Very soon a funeral director will set up a system where you will be able to arrange a funeral and accomplish it all online.

Here are important links where you can find help.

- The entire Funeral Rule online:
  http://ftc.gov/bcp/conline/pubs/services/funeral.htm

- The Veterans Administration:
  www.cem.va.gov

There are more items online that can help you lower your funeral cost at the following websites.

- Get 7 — the seven secrets of funeral cash, and access to a funeral director here: http://www.LowerCostFuneral.com

- Get up-to-date funeral information here: http://www.LowerCostFuneral.blogr.com

- An audio version of this book is available at: http://www.SecretFuneralCash.com

- For memorial folders/cards of any kind for your funeral: http://www.LovedOnesGreetings.com

These are the best and most inexpensive ways to build memorial websites:

- www.EZMiniSites.com

- www.7MinuteWebsites.com

- www.Ellisera.com

These are two very effective places to promote the legacy of your loved one. The people behind these links have big hearts. They may even help you pay for the funeral.

- www.InternetMarketingDreams.com

- www.PromotingTips.com

Some of the best funeral information can be found at:

- http://www.RBrianBurkhardt.com

For flowers and caskets, search "wholesale flowers" and "wholesale caskets" on the internet to open up a variety of discount choices.

My Gifts To You
To Help In Your
Time Of Need

The author will give you **$377 worth of free gifts** for buying this book. This includes 15 minutes on the phone with a Funeral Director, his popular download, and his Lower Cost Funeral E-Newsletter, Proof of Purchase and an Email address is required. Get the three bonuses here:

www.LowerCostFuneral.com/3bonuses.htm

The author realizes that some people will need personalized attention. He has an event called "LiveFD." (FUNERAL DONE.) One is required to read this book and go through a short phone interview to attend. These events fill up fast. No funeral goods/services are sold. At "LiveFD" we will help you plan Your Own Low Cost Less Stress Funeral. We do realize that planning your funeral is probably the most private personal thing you will ever do. CONFIDENCES are strictly kept. R. Brian adheres to the strictest Funeral Ethics. What you share with him stays with him. A select few are accepted in these events. Go Here:

www.LowerCostFuneral.com/FDevent.htm

The author has the unique ability to leverage his experience to lower the cost of your Funeral. He welcomes your feedback. R. Brian can take funeral information: the taboo not thought of, overwhelming and mystical — boil it down to the core essence — and help you with your low cost funeral. He delivers insider unknown processes and is available for speaking engagements, seminars and consulting. He will speak at your local Red Hat Society or community organization. He approaches each funeral with respect and care. He is your Funeral Advocate. Go here:

www.LowerCostFuneral.com/communicate.htm